Three Mills – the Clock Mill and House Mill, Lee Navigation. The third mill disappeared long ago.

London's Canals

Derek Pratt

A Shire book

Published in 2004 by Shire Publications Ltd,
Cromwell House, Church Street, Princes Risborough,
Buckinghamshire HP27 9AA, UK.
(Website: www.shirebooks.co.uk)

Copyright © 2004 by Derek Pratt.
First published 1977 as 'Discovering London's Canals'.
Second edition 1981. Third edition 1987. Fourth edition,
revised and updated in colour as a Shire Album, 2004.
Shire Album 432. ISBN 0 7478 0601 2.
Derek Pratt is hereby identified as the author of this work
in accordance with Section 77 of the Copyright, Designs
and Patents Act 1988.

British Library Cataloguing in Publication Data:
Pratt, Derek
London's canals. – 4th ed. – (Shire album; 432)
1. Canals – England – London – Guidebooks
2. London (England) – Guidebooks
I. Title II. Pratt, Derek.
Discovering London's canals 914.2'1
ISBN 0 7478 0601 2.

Cover: *Jason's Trip passing Snowdon's Aviary, London Zoo.*

ACKNOWLEDGEMENTS
I would like to thank Amanda Moring at British Waterways, Paddington Office, for all
the help and information she gave me regarding new developments on London's canals.
I am also indebted to the Internet, which enabled me to find information (however
obscure), thus saving me interminable and expensive telephone calls.
Cartography by Richard G. Holmes. Photography by the author.

Printed in Malta by Gutenberg Press Limited, Gudja Road,
Tarxien PLA 19, Malta

Contents

London's other waterway

The River Thames is one of the world's best-known rivers and without it London would probably not have existed. The city first took shape on the banks of the river, gradually spreading out as its population and prosperity increased. During the eighteenth century the Industrial Revolution caused the expansion of towns and cities in other parts of Britain. London was left virtually out of touch with the new manufacturing centres in the Midlands and the North. Cities such as Birmingham and Sheffield had no major river by which to transport their manufactured goods or receive raw materials; the only method of transport was via primitive roads that were no better than rutted, potholed tracks, making it almost impossible to bring in raw materials and safely distribute finished goods. It was essential for the manufacturing towns to be linked to the ports and the solution was to build canals.

The first canal to be independent of a river was built near Manchester by the Duke of Bridgewater in 1761. Afterwards the introduction of the pound lock made it possible for canals to negotiate gradients – although the early canal engineers tended to follow land contours whenever possible. In the following fifty years canals were constructed all over Britain.

The Oxford Canal (completed in 1790) made the first connection between the industrial areas of the Midlands and the North and the River Thames. For the boatman an arduous journey down-river from Oxford to the capital still remained. London's first direct link with the waterways of the Midlands began with the construction of the Grand Junction Canal at the turn of the nineteenth century. The link with the Thames at Brentford was complete by 1800, cutting over 60 miles (100 km) off the earlier journey via Oxford and avoiding the necessity for transhipment to barges. The new Grand Junction locks were twice the width of those on the narrow Oxford Canal – which meant they could take wide barges or two narrowboats side by side. Soon the Paddington Arm brought the Grand Junction Canal nearer to central London, followed by the building of the Regent's Canal in 1820, providing an east London outlet to the river. Although the canals arrived relatively late in London, commerce via the waterways lasted longer in the capital than in many other parts of Britain when faced with railway competition. Three million tons of cargo were moved on London's canals in 1924. Coal, timber, sand, gravel and groceries were the main cargoes at that time.

The River Lee Navigation starts at Hertford and takes a southerly route through north and east London to join the Thames at Canning Town. It has two direct links with the Regent's Canal, which runs from Limehouse to Paddington. The Paddington Arm heads out across north-west London to Southall, where it joins the main line at Bulls Bridge. There is a branch near Uxbridge that runs to Slough. The main line continues through Uxbridge and heads out over the Chiltern Hills to Birmingham and the rest of England. From the centre of London it is possible to travel by boat to places as far afield as Lincoln, Llangollen, Gloucester and Goole. Major cities such as Manchester, Leeds, Nottingham, Bristol and Coventry are all accessible by canal from London.

There was considerably more green countryside to be seen when London's canals were first built. Suburbs such as Hanwell and Southall were mere villages separated by farms and fields. The canal attracted industry to its banks. Factories and foundries were built with waterside wharves where boats could load and unload their cargoes. The canals continued to function as busy commercial waterways right up to the 1960s, carrying such varied cargoes as coal, timber, sand, chemicals and domestic rubbish. The shipment of raw lime juice in barrels from Brentford to Rose's factory at Apsley in Hertfordshire, which finished in 1981, was the last regular commercial narrowboat run on the southern Grand Union until 2003, when a gravel barge contract began operating between Denham and West Drayton.

The people who worked the narrowboats had a way of life that was totally dependent on the canals. They had to labour extremely hard, especially in winter when the water was frozen. The boatman and his family lived and slept in the tiny cramped cabins behind the cargo hold at the back of the boats. Because they were an itinerant community they were often regarded with suspicion by land-based people and so became isolated from the rest of society. With the decline of trade, the families gradually

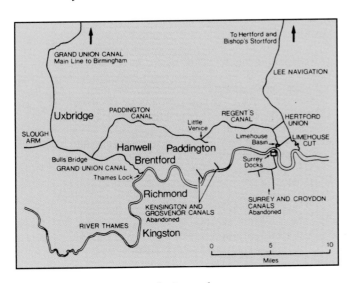

London's canals.

Moorings at Blomfield Road, Little Venice, Regent's Canal.

drifted away from the canal to work in factories or to retirement. A few did manage to stay on as lock-keepers or maintenance men.

The canal is commemorated by the names of streets and pubs around the city. Besides Canal Street and Wharf Road there is Praed Street in Paddington named after William Praed, the first chairman of the Grand Junction Canal Company. Pub signs include the Grand Junction Arms, the Narrow Boat, the Pleasure Boat and the Paddington Packet Boat.

Most of the boats now seen on London's canals are privately owned or are public trip boats. Most of the trip boats are to be found on the very popular section of canal between Little Venice and Camden Lock. Indeed, arriving at London Zoo by boat is by far the most attractive way to see the animals.

Hired holiday boats from outside the capital are often seen during the summer months. In 2004 there were no boats for holiday hire in the London area but a plan was underway for a fleet of hire boats to operate from the new marina at Cowley Peachey.

In 1968, Westminster City Council was the first local authority to provide a canal walk for public use. This ran between

Primrose Hill and Lisson Grove. Before this walkway opened the public had been actively discouraged from using the towpath, with access often denied at bridges. All the canal towpaths are now open and their use is both encouraged and promoted. Hidden beneath the towpath are electricity and fibre-optic cables, which bring in revenue to British Waterways. Information boards about the canal and its history are displayed in many places.

There are many changes occurring alongside London's canals. In 2004 there were major developments in progress at Paddington and Brentford. On the Paddington Canal there was extensive construction work taking place at the former Heinz, Lyons and Taylor-Woodrow sites. Limehouse Basin had been completed, but the Channel Tunnel link project will cause some changes to the canal at St Pancras. There will be big changes on the lower Lee Navigation should London be successful in its bid for the 2012 Olympic Games.

London's canals are now part of the Grand Union Canal system and the River Lee Navigation, both owned and managed by British Waterways. There are traces of other canals to be found but these are long abandoned and mostly infilled.

This book is for people who want to discover the canals of London on foot or by boat. Most people's awareness of the canal ends at Camden Lock or London Zoo at Regent's Park, but there are about 60 miles (100 km) of London's waterways waiting to be explored by visitors who want to look further than the obvious tourist attractions. All the walks described in this book are north of the Thames.

The Grand Union main line, Brentford to Denham

The Grand Junction Canal between Brentford and Uxbridge was opened in November 1794 with celebrations and processions along its length. At that time the present Brentford Lock was the last one on the canal and boats were subject to delay in navigating the tidal Brent Creek. The Thames Lock was eventually constructed once opposition from millers using the water on the creek had been overcome. The River Brent joins the main line at the bottom of Hanwell Locks and is then canalised down to the Thames at Brentford.

In 1929 the Grand Junction main-line canal was amalgamated with the Paddington Arm, the Regent's Canal and all the lines to Birmingham, Leicester and near Nottingham to form the Grand Union Canal. The new Grand Union Canal became the most extensive canal in Britain and carried an immense quantity of goods. Railway competition eventually affected the overall tonnages – although the Grand Union did not suffer as much as did some other waterways. Brentford with its transhipment

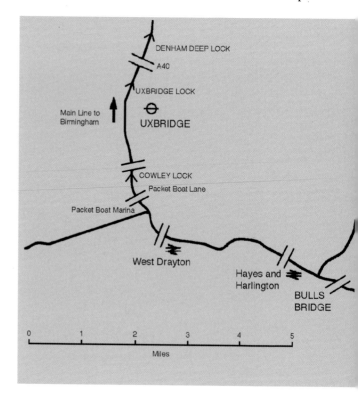

depot remained a very busy terminal to the canal until the 1970s. At the start of the twenty-first century there are big changes afoot in the Brentford area so it is here that we shall begin our walk.

From Brentford station (National Rail from Waterloo), turn left along Boston Manor Road, continuing along Half Acre and turning left along High Street, then right into Dock Road.

Start at Thames Lock, which is to be found at the end of the cobbled Dock Road opposite Somerfield supermarket and the Beehive pub. There are two locks standing side by side on the tidal Brent Creek. This is the start of the Grand Union Canal, whose entrance from the Thames faces Kew Gardens. The locks are operated by a resident lock-keeper and boat access is dependent on the state of the tide. The second lock was added and both were electrified in 1962, when the creek was busy with barges and lighters. The former Brentford Railway Dock has its own separate entrance to the Thames. It is now used by a marina that is surrounded by a large housing development. The marina can be seen at the end of Dock Road beyond Thames Lock.

Walk down the steps to the footpath on the left of the locks and proceed until you reach a footbridge. Across the water can be

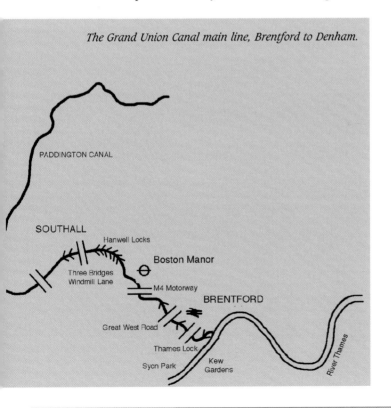

The Grand Union Canal main line, Brentford to Denham.

seen a number of boatyards with a miscellany of craft ranging from canal boats to sea-going cruisers. Cross the footbridge and follow the path into Brent Way. Here you can either follow the sign for the Thames Path, which will lead to the canal bridge, or take an alternative route and turn right (do not pass under the railway bridge). If following the alternative route, just after a bend in the road turn left down an alley behind the Magpie and Crown pub. This takes you to Brentford High Street, where you should cross the road to the magistrates' court. Behind the court buildings in a narrow street is the White Horse (just one of several fine pubs to be found near the canal in Brentford). A plaque on the wall tells you that this was once the home of the artist J. M. W. Turner (1775–1851). Turn left at the pub into Market Place, which leads to The Butts with its fine Georgian houses. Here on the left, almost hidden behind trees, is the Boatmen's Institute (1904), founded to care for the boat people and to educate their children.

Return to the High Street, turn right and walk to the canal bridge. You will see Brentford Gauging Locks and the toll-house where traffic coming from the Thames was assessed for the value of its cargo.

Beyond the locks you would have seen the warehouses of Brentford Transhipment Depot until their demolition in 2003. The depot was once a bustling scene of industry with barges and lighters from the Thames mingling with canal boats. Cranes would have been loading and unloading all types of cargo from one craft to another or into lorries. Following the decline of canal trade in the early 1960s the depot continued to operate as a storage place for freight from the Thames. By the mid 1980s this trade had ceased and the depot fell into disuse. In 2004 the old depot site was being transformed by the construction of 350 new houses and a large hotel. There were also plans for a piazza area with waterside bars and restaurants, a new wetland area for wildlife, and improved flood protection measures on the river section.

Walk down to the footpath to the left of the Gauging Locks and cross over a footbridge. Soon you will see the first of the Grand Junction Canal mileposts, telling you that Braunston is 93 miles (150 km) away. Although Braunston is a village near Daventry in Northamptonshire it is the hub of the canal system south of Birmingham. It has long been an important canal centre for working boats and pleasure boating, and it has a junction with the Oxford Canal.

The path disappears into a huge canopied warehouse that is the only survivor from the heyday of the old depot. This is where perishable cargoes could be safely handled away from the vagaries of the weather.

There are a number of modern office buildings near the Great West Road bridge, all impressive in their own right but totally overshadowed by the glass cathedral-like Glaxo Smith Kline building. This is an enormous structure dominating both the

Passing the Glaxo building at Great West Road, Brentford.

road and the canal. There is a landscaped area with a modern sculpture and seats where workers can sit out by the canal in their leisure time.

A wooden footbridge takes you into Boston Manor Park, where there is a seventeenth-century manor house and gardens.

Clitheroe's Lock was probably named after former owners of Boston Manor. Beyond it roars the elevated M4 motorway above the River Brent. The motorway soon bends away towards Heathrow and the canal passes under Gallows Bridge. Built in the Midlands by the Horseley Iron Works, this is one of the finest canal bridges in the south of England. Cast-iron bridges of this type are very common around the canals of the West Midlands but are rarely found this far south. The bridge has been painted and the anomaly of 'Grand Union Canal 1820' rectified. The original inscription correctly read 'Grand Junction Canal' but was later foolishly altered to 'Grand Union Canal', a name that did not exist until 1929. This is a turnover bridge designed to enable boat horses to cross the canal when the towpath changes sides.

The Heathrow branch of the Piccadilly Line of the London Underground crosses the canal on a high metal bridge. Soon afterwards the canal passes under the M4 motorway and arrives at Osterley Lock. The lock is situated next to mature woodland between the canal and the River Brent and only the noise of the motorway traffic disturbs the tranquillity of the scene. Look for the charming mosaics set in brickwork on the ground beside the lock and made by children from a nearby school.

Beyond the lock the River Brent leaves the canal and plunges over a large toothed weir. Rising sharply behind the river is the Elthorne extension, which has playing fields and wildlife reserves. A large sculpture of a deer (known locally as the 'Elthorne Bambi') can be seen at the top of the slope, rather incongruously set next to a football pitch. *This is the nearest point to Boston Manor station (Underground, Piccadilly Line). To reach it, cross pitches to Southdown Avenue, turn right to the end of the avenue, then left into the main road. The station is on the right.*

A pleasant half-mile amble takes you to Hanwell Locks. The River Brent enters the canal under a bridge on the towpath side just before the bottom lock. The Fox pub can be found a short distance along the lane before the bridge. In 1897 the Brent was so polluted it was described as an open sewer and boatmen complained of the stench caused by filth stirred up by their loaded boats. These days a

Hanwell Bottom Lock.

resident heron and the occasional kingfisher are living proof that
fish have returned to the Brent.

There are several splendid walks around here. Jubilee Meadow
and Blackberry Corner, unspoilt wild spaces, can be found by
crossing the lock. Here one can well imagine the open
countryside common to this area before the locks were built in
1794. Next to the towpath is another path indicating the
entrance to Fitzherbert Walk, part of the Brent River Park, which
runs for 6 miles (10 km) between the A40 Western Avenue and
Brentford High Street.

A walk to Bunny Park

At the bottom lock follow the Fitzherbert Walk by the River Brent to Hanwell Bridge. Cross the road under a pedestrian subway and carry on into Brent Meadow with the river on your right. The Wharncliffe or Hanwell railway viaduct looms up in front of you. This was built by Isambard Kingdom Brunel in 1837 and carries the Great Western Railway from Paddington to the West Country. Cross the river over a little bridge directly underneath the viaduct and pass through a gate into a steep grassy area known as Churchfields. *To reach Hanwell station, walk up the slope and turn right at the top. Follow a track between a public garden and the railway viaduct to a road junction. Go straight ahead along Golden Manor and turn right into Campbell Road. Follow this to the end and bear right to the station entrance.* To continue the walk to Bunny Park, go up the slope and turn left along a beautiful avenue of chestnut trees to St Mary's Church, which was built by Gilbert Scott. Turn left in front of the church and enter Brent Lodge Park (popularly known as the 'Bunny Park'). Follow the path to a zoo, where there is an excellent café, a Millennium maze and an adventure playground. Return to the canal by the same route.

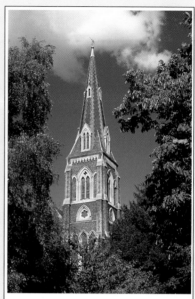

The spire of St Mary's Church, Hanwell.

Back at the canal, there are six locks in the Hanwell Flight, raising the canal by 53 feet (16 metres). Around 60,000 gallons (270,000 litres) are lost at each lock with every boat movement up the flight. A high wall on the towpath side separates the canal from Ealing Hospital grounds and the former St Bernard's mental hospital. Note the bricked-up arch in the wall between Locks 93 and 94. This was once the entrance to Asylum Dock through which boats delivered coal for the hospital's boilers. Lock 94 is still known as 'Asylum Lock'. The red-painted doors set into the wall are fire doors that allowed fire engines to extract water from the canal if a blaze occurred in the hospital. Sometimes a boat horse would slip into the water when pulling a heavy load so horse ramps helped them escape from the steep-sided canal; these can still be seen at Hanwell Locks.

The next bridge is the renowned 'Three Bridges', where road, rail and canal cross at the same point at different levels. Three Bridges is actually one bridge and an aqueduct. Brunel built the railway in 1859 and a section of his broad-gauge rail can be seen acting as a bridge guard on the southern side of the aqueduct.

Only the garden wall survives of the fine lock cottage at Lock 91. The cottage was demolished but remains undeveloped and the debris is overgrown with weeds and wild flowers. A small sculpture of a steam-driven canal boat in a lock is inaccurate and out of proportion. It stands by the entrance to Glade Lane open space, where there are adventure facilities for older children.

A splendid whitewashed bridge frames the entrance to Norwood Top Lock, where British Waterways has an office and maintenance yard. Now begins a long lock-free pound stretching to Cowley Lock near Uxbridge on the main line and along the Paddington and Regent's Canals as far as Camden Lock. Add to this the Slough Arm (see page 21) and there is a distance of around 27 miles (43 km) of water uninterrupted by locks. Note the lock and bridge competition plaques indicating that the lock has won prizes for being well kept.

After the lock the towpath rises over the entrance to the Maypole Arm, which runs for half a mile to Maypole Dock. It was built in 1913 to serve the Monsted margarine works and later the Quaker Oats factory. In 2004 it was being used for private moorings and was not open to the public.

A long straight stretch leads to the Lamb pub, which has a waterside garden and stands next to a busy main road. A

Norwood Top Lock, Grand Union main line. This specially adapted narrowboat, owned by Wyvern Shipping Company at Linslade, Bedfordshire, was on its way to become the first canal boat to reach the Scilly Isles. It returned via the Bristol Channel, re-entering the inland waterway system at Bristol and travelling via the Avon Navigation and the Kennet & Avon Canal.

milepost opposite the pub reads 'Braunston 89 miles'. In the past Adelaide Dock was a bustling boatyard full of floating and dry-docked boats being built, repaired and maintained. In 2004 it was, sadly, standing disused, but there were high expectations that it would one day return to being an active boatyard.

The Old Oak Tree pub stands opposite a brick humpback bridge and old terraced cottages flank the adjoining road. The next section of canal, between the Grand Junction Arms and Bulls Bridge, has a quiet road running parallel to it that is often used in film and television dramas.

The elegant, whitewashed Bulls Bridge marks the start of the Paddington Canal and the water route to central London. It once faced a lively scene of working narrowboats at the Grand Union Canal Company offices and repair yards. Dozens of boats with their smoking chimneys were moored here while the boatmen awaited orders for their next job. The women would take advantage of the luxury of running water and do the family wash while the children had a schoolroom in an old barge. In later years the site became a repair and maintenance depot for British Waterways. A modern sculpture beneath Bulls Bridge commemorates the people who lived and worked on the canals and who developed their own unique community with its own costumes and customs. The bridge now faces a huge Tesco supermarket built on the site of the old depot. The supermarket has mooring facilities and a restaurant and is a popular stopping place for visiting boaters wishing to stock up their larder. There are moorings further along the canal – some

Bulls Bridge Junction, Grand Union main line.

of them for permanent houseboats – and also a dry-dock facility.

Beyond Bulls Bridge the busy Hayes Bypass noisily crosses the canal on concrete pillars. The large factory on the offside of the canal is occupied by Nestlé and was called 'Hayes Chocolate' by the working boatmen. The company no longer uses canal transport, leaving a long wharf deserted of any commercial activity.

The towpath rises over a short arm once known as 'Shackle's Dock' as the canal passes through Hayes town centre, with its abundance of shops and pubs. *Turn left over the canal bridge to reach Hayes & Harlington station (National Rail from Paddington), nearby. From the station entrance, turn right to reach the canal bridge.* The canal continues westward in a shallow cutting through an industrial area largely screened by trees and bushes. Most bridges have an attendant pub.

At Stockley Bridge you may be lucky enough to see a barge unloading gravel and aggregates – a rare example of current commercial use of the lower Grand Union Canal. Bridge 195 is adjacent to the Stockley Park Science Park and Stockley Country Park, both constructed on 400 acres (162 hectares) of formerly derelict land. This was once the heart of the brickfields industry, where numerous docks were built to transport bricks and gravel to Paddington and Brentford. The boats would return filled with domestic rubbish to use as landfill in the quarries.

The factory occupying both sides of the canal at Horton Bridge has a landscaped water frontage. The whitewashed humpback

A view of Bulls Bridge Junction from Tesco moorings.

A milepost at Cowley Peachey Junction, Grand Union main line.

bridge is fringed with willows and shrubs. The railway is very close to the canal and soon you will see a group of rail-to-water transhipment sheds on the offside of the canal.

West Drayton station *(National Rail from Paddington) is next to the canal at Bridge 192.* Shops and pubs are close by. Another factory with a long canalside wharf has been demolished. Soon you will see the entrance to the Slough Arm at Cowley Peachey Junction. A great deal of landscaping has been carried out here since the building of Packet Boat Marina, and seating has been provided close by the bridge. Packet Boat Marina, with a capacity for 120 boats, was opened in 2003 and is owned by British Waterways. It has a café that is open to the public.

The old wharf area at Bridge 190 accommodates the Turning Point pub and restaurant. Diners and drinkers overlook moorings and the bridge of a former canal arm that now has a fountain. This was the terminus of Packet Boat Dock, from where the horse-drawn Paddington Packet Boat once ran a passenger service to Paddington, 15 miles (24 km) away. The nearby Paddington Packet Boat Inn at the end of the lane commemorates this service, which operated at the beginning of the nineteenth century.

Cowley Lock, Grand Union main line.

Lines of moorings lead to a whitewashed bridge and then to Cowley Lock. This marks the end of a long lock-free section (known as a 'pound') that stretches from Camden Lock and Norwood Top Lock. An attractive group of cottages leads to a popular pub and restaurant by the bridge. The former toll-house is now a tearoom.

Industrial estates dominate both sides of the canal as a long line of moorings brings you into the rather drab outskirts of Uxbridge. The General Elliot pub is situated on the canal and has a terrace that faces the Uxbridge Boat Centre on the opposite bank. This is one of several boatyards in the Uxbridge area. Uxbridge was once was the home of the famous canal carrying company Fellows, Morton & Clayton. Narrowboats were registered here and the legend 'Registered at Uxbridge' can still be seen on old working boats. Uxbridge town centre has sold its soul to the motor car but nevertheless bits of the old place can still be seen and there are some notable pubs such as the historic Crown and Treaty. The Swan and Bottle by the main road bridge was once a favourite stopping place for boatmen.

To reach Uxbridge station (Underground, Metropolitan and Piccadilly Lines), turn right up the High Street. To reach the canal from Uxbridge station, leave by the High Street exit and turn right down to the canal bridge.

An extraordinary Art Deco style building in green and cream that resembles a beached ocean liner now overlooks the old pub. There is a complex series of backwaters and a large flour mill at Uxbridge Lock. An attractive whitewashed roving bridge in front of the lock completes the scene. The last vestiges of London are left behind as the canal heads out into open countryside. Just

The Grand Union main line at Denham.

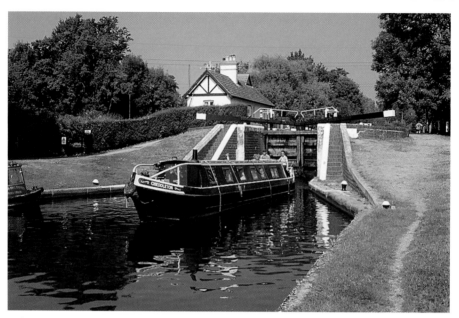

A boat leaving Denham Deep Lock, Grand Union main line.

beyond the wide M40 bridge is a wharf built in 2003 at which barges are loaded with sand and gravel from a conveyor.

Denham Country Park can be reached a few yards before Denham Deep Lock, where Fran's Tea Garden can be found behind the pretty lock cottage next to the river and canal. Sitting in this idyllic garden it is hard to believe that junction 1 of the M40 motorway is only half a mile or so away. Fran's is an ideal place to end this journey along the Grand Union main line.

Denham station (National Rail from Marylebone) can be reached from Denham Lock (a walk of about 1½ miles) by following a public footpath that leaves the towpath a short distance south of the lock. On coming to a road, keep forward past Denham Country Park Visitor Centre. Then cross a golf course to a road in Denham village. Turn right past the church until it bends to the left by a large house. From here a footpath on the right will bring you to the railway station. There are three pubs in Denham village. There is parking for cars at Denham Country Park Visitor Centre, with a short walk across the fields to the canal.

The Slough Arm

The 5 miles (8 km) long Slough Arm was built in 1882, making it one of the last canals to be completed in Britain. It has three aqueducts but no locks and is virtually dead straight from beginning to end. The main purpose of its construction was to transport bricks used in London's expansion in the late Victorian era. When the brickfields were eventually exhausted, gravel became an important commodity in keeping the canal commercially active.

The first part of the canal is green and wooded and passes over the three aqueducts. This is a very watery area with three rivers and flooded gravel pits much frequented by anglers. The entrance to the new marina by the main line at Cowley Peachey is from the Slough Arm. A footbridge has been built and the surroundings have been landscaped. The canal runs into a wooded cutting after passing under the M25 motorway. It skirts around an industrial estate on the outskirts of Iver and follows a pleasant green course to Mansion Lane, where High Line Yachting has a large boatyard. A long line of linear moorings takes the canal to Langley, in which there are shops and a station. The canal becomes increasingly built up with housing and industrial estates as it approaches Slough. It ends rather ignominiously by a builder's merchant screened by reeds and bushes from the main road. The entrance is almost opposite the Nag's Head pub. The Slough Arm was once part of an ambitious plan to link the Grand Union Canal to the River Thames at Maidenhead. Some optimists believe this scheme is still possible.

The entrance to Packet Boat Marina, Slough Arm.

Turn left along the road to reach Slough station (National Rail from Paddington).

Linear moorings on the Slough Arm at Langley.

The Paddington Canal

The Paddington Canal – or, more correctly, the Paddington Arm of the Grand Junction Canal – was opened in July 1801. It provided a direct link from the Grand Junction main line into central London, thus avoiding the River Thames.

The 13 miles (21 km) long canal between Bulls Bridge, Southall, and Paddington was built on one level and so boats made rapid progress unhindered by locks. Industry swiftly developed on its banks, taking full advantage of the fast method of transport. Companies built their own wharves and private docks and at its terminus Paddington developed into a thriving inland port. In its commercial heyday Paddington Basin was flanked with warehouses and the pool was crammed with boats both loading and discharging all types of goods. Horses were everywhere, pulling carts and drays or resting in the many stables dotted around the basin. Smells from the horses and the barges full of domestic rubbish would have been overwhelming. There would have been piles of sand, gravel, bricks and horse manure that had to be shifted manually. Local pubs such as the Grand Junction Arms would have been full of boatmen having a drink before starting work on the next load. Paddington Basin was also the terminus of the Paddington Packet Boat passenger service from Cowley near Uxbridge (see page 18). The basin lost some of its trade to the Regent's Canal when that was built in 1820 and later, like most canals, suffered from railway competition. It did, however, remain quite busy until the end of

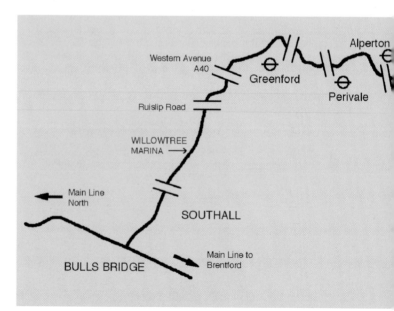

the Second World War. Gradually the basin went into decline and became a rubbish-filled backwater without public access. It is surprising that this large expanse of water, less than a mile from Marble Arch, remained unused and derelict for so long.

In 2004 there were three developments underway at Paddington. The first, Paddington Central, was almost complete at the time of writing. Built on the former Paddington Station goods yard, it will be a mixed-use development with offices, retail space and over two hundred apartments. A landscaped public arena is to feature exhibitions and entertainment, as well as a number of interesting modern sculptures, and there will be waterside restaurants and bars. The second development involves the transformation of the old Paddington Basin into Paddington Waterside and is one of the biggest urban regeneration schemes in Europe. At the time of writing the basin was an immense building site with tall blocks still under construction. When completed it will have homes, offices, shops, bars, cafés and a hotel. There are proposals for floating offices and a floating classroom. Public access (so long denied) will be encouraged. New pedestrian bridges were also being constructed, including the unique Helix Bridge that is designed to rotate and retract on a steel corkscrew, allowing boats to pass through. This short glass tunnel will connect West End Quay to the Paddington Health Campus. The third development, still in its planning stages in 2004, will be a new waterside concourse to Paddington Station intended to open up the station's gloomy north side with a glass-built entrance giving direct access to the canal.

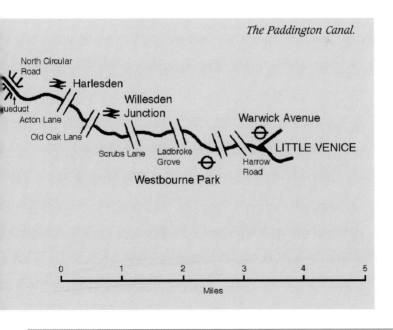

The Paddington Canal.

The Helix bridge at Paddington Basin.

Start at Little Venice (*nearest station Warwick Avenue: Underground, Bakerloo Line*), which is a triangular-shaped pool with a tree-fringed island and is the junction of the Paddington and Regent's Canals. The island is known as 'Browning's Island' after the poet Robert Browning, who lived nearby. One side of the pool is flanked by the Rembrandt Gardens, where you can sit among the summer flowers and watch a busy waterside scene. Public trip boats carry passengers to London Zoo and Camden Lock and there are usually interesting canal boats to be seen on the moorings. There is a permanent floating art gallery, a conference and exhibition barge and a floating café. A regular boat service operating from Little Venice to London Zoo includes the entrance fee to the zoo.

Visit Little Venice during the bank-holiday weekend at the beginning of May and you will see a huge gathering of boats celebrating the Canalway Cavalcade. This annual three-day event has become a popular feature of the London boating scene.

At one end of the pool, the Regent's Canal begins its journey to Limehouse under a fine cast-iron bridge by the flower garden.

Little Venice during the Canalway Cavalcade.

At the other end of the garden the entrance to the old Paddington Basin can be seen beneath the elevated Westway motorway. Beyond the motorway bridge, a footbridge over the canal will take you to the Paddington Central development. From there follow signs to Paddington station.

The third point of the triangle has a cast-iron footbridge that marks the start of the Paddington Canal. On the left, just beyond the bridge, is the Toll Office, known to the working boatmen as 'Paddington Stop'. Boats were stopped here to have the weight of their cargoes gauged and to be issued with toll tickets. It was once a very busy place with toll clerks working in shifts throughout the day and into the night. The office is now the London headquarters of British Waterways.

Delamere Terrace is lined with a miscellany of moored craft and houseboats on both sides of the canal. Among them is the starting point of Jason's Trip boat, which is in Blomfield Road and is reached either from Little Venice or over the concrete footbridge ahead. Jason's Trip takes passengers along the Regent's Canal to Camden Lock and has been operating from here since 1951. It has a restaurant specialising in seafood, and restaurant boats are also available for hire.

The large housing complex on the towpath side is called the Warwick and Brindley Estate. Presumably this is a tribute to James Brindley, the pioneer canal engineer – who had no connection with the Grand Junction Canal and was dead before any canal reached London. St Mary Magdalene Church, with its soaring spire, was built in the Victorian era and is now surrounded by the modern estate.

Note the rope grooving on the cast-iron bridge plates at Harrow Road Bridge. In the days of the working boats, constant chafing of the horses' wet towing ropes gradually ate into the metal guards. Similar examples can be seen throughout the canal system.

The next section of canal is dominated by the soaring elevated Westway motorway that sweeps over the canal on its way to Oxford and Birmingham. Four generations of transport – the Great Western Railway, the Metropolitan Railway, the Westway motorway and the Paddington Canal – all converge at this point.

Carlton Bridge is a fine cast-iron structure with an adjoining pub and is *close to Westbourne Park Underground station (Hammersmith & City Line)*. Look out for some very adroit and hair-raising skateboard antics by young people at the Carlton Bridge adventure playground. The canal runs parallel to Harrow Road, along which a new housing development is followed by old terraced houses. The canal is overlooked by a thirty-storey monolithic tower block that is one of the tallest buildings in west London and is visible for miles around. It is unlikely that concrete blocks such as this will ever be built again and indeed there is a possibility that this particular building will be preserved for all time as an example of 1960s municipal housing. The Meanwhile Wildlife Garden is a welcome piece of greenery to be found directly beneath the tower. Another narrow strip of garden has been created between the canal and Harrow Road, giving passengers on the upper deck of buses their first view of the hitherto hidden canal.

In 1819 the area around Ladbroke Grove, then called Plough Lane, was described as 'a beautiful burst of scenery with distant views of the Hampstead Hills' (John Hassell, *A Tour of the Grand Junction Canal*). This rural idyll has long since disappeared under brick and concrete. Present-day visitors to Ladbroke Grove at the end of August would be advised to wear earplugs as protection against the cacophony of the Notting Hill Carnival, which usually starts near the canal bridge.

The towpath rises sharply over the entrance to Kensal Wharf, also known as 'Port-A-Bella-Dock'. This was once a council disposal centre for household rubbish and ashes, which were carried by boat to Hayes and West Drayton to fill up the holes in the quarries and brickfields. During the Second World War the dock was drained and used to store sand for sandbags. The arches of the wharf provided shelter for air-raid rescue squads.

Moorings by the supermarket at Ladbroke Grove, Paddington Canal.

In February 1944 the wharf was bombed and some of the original buildings were destroyed.

The futuristic building on the other side of Ladbroke Bridge is a cable monitoring station for the national grid. Beyond that, with moorings and access from the towpath, is a large Sainsbury's supermarket with a coffee shop by the canal entrance. Survivors and the injured were brought here after the Ladbroke Grove train crash in October 1999. Next to Sainsbury's is a water-based activity and recreation centre for young people.

Continuing westwards, the towpath rises steeply over the entrance to the private dock of the now defunct Kensal Green gasworks. Over the years huge quantities of coal from the Midlands coalfields were delivered here. The last working boat to use the dock was a tar barge from the gasworks to Beckton in east London in 1957. The late Victorian gasholders have some fine wrought-iron tracery that is best seen silhouetted against a sunset.

Kensal Green Cemetery flanks the offside of the canal between Ladbroke Grove and Scrubs Lane. This enormous graveyard,

covering an area of 56 acres (23 hectares), was opened in 1833. There is a gate from the canal to the cemetery so it is likely that some souls made their final journey by water. Among the many celebrated people buried here are the engineer Isambard Kingdom Brunel and the writers Anthony Trollope, William Thackeray and Wilkie Collins. This is also the last resting place of the actor Charles Kemble and of Charles Blondin, the tightrope walker. The cemetery has many trees and bushes, providing a welcome sanctuary for birds and other wildlife.

The Great Western Railway runs parallel to the canal for some distance. After Mitre Bridge, which carries Scrubs Lane over the canal, you can see the many tracks of the railway marshalling yards. In the days of steam these were the Old Oak Common

Passing Kensal Green Cemetery, Paddington Canal.

engine sheds. Beyond the railway is the wide expanse of Wormwood Scrubs, with the famous prison and Hammersmith Hospital in the background. Several pioneer aviators made early flying sorties on the grassy open spaces of Wormwood Scrubs at the beginning of the twentieth century.

Willesden Junction station (Underground, Bakerloo Line; National Rail from Euston and North London Line) is close to the canal at Old Oak Bridge amid a tangle of railways. The nearby Fisherman's Arms provides refreshment for the thirsty. Industry returns with the bright yellow cranes of the Euro Terminal, formerly the Willesden Freightliner Depot.

Bushes, trees and a sloping grassy embankment soften the industrial landscape as the canal passes Acton Lane Power Station, which was once a major user of the canal for coal supplies. Water from the canal is used in the power station's cooling cycle.

At Acton Lane the Grand Junction Arms pub has a waterside frontage with a garden and moorings for visiting boats. It is pleasantly situated among the factories of the Park Royal Industrial Estate. There is a café opposite the Grand Junction Arms and *Harlesden station (Underground, Bakerloo Line; National Rail from Euston) is just around the corner.* Workers from the industrial estate make good use of the towpath seating during their lunch breaks as the area around the towpath has been landscaped with bushes and flowering shrubs. A feeder stream from Brent Reservoir emerges from beneath a little bridge on the offside of the canal.

Large munitions factories were built at Park Royal during the First World War and the present industrial estate developed on the site afterwards. Famous companies such as Guinness and Heinz opened factories that used the canal extensively for bringing in raw materials and distributing the finished products afterwards. In 1923 Park Royal Estate had seventy-three factories employing 13,400 people. The Guinness Brewery had its own wharf that shipped beer by canal. Heinz had a huge factory emblazoned with the number '57' on its office block. It opened in 1925 and was demolished in 2002. Heinz used the canal to bring in raw beans and tomato purée from the docks and boats would carry canned goods away from the factory. The site, with its long canal frontage, was standing undeveloped in 2004. The *Radio Times* was

The North Circular Aqueduct, Paddington Canal.

published in a building behind the lengthman's cottage until 1984.

North Circular Aqueduct is around a bend in the canal shortly after the lengthman's cottage. The original structure, built in 1830, was demolished when the road was widened. The new extended concrete aqueduct splits into twin channels as it crosses the busy road. It gives boaters and walkers a rare opportunity to view the traffic jams below. More factories and light industrial estates appear on both sides as the canal crosses the River Brent and moves into Alperton.

There is another large waterside Sainsbury's supermarket near the road bridge at Alperton. The Pleasure Boat pub has a garden next to the canal and *Alperton Underground station (Piccadilly Line) is over the bridge.* Willow trees hang attractively over the water and a garishly painted office-block tower overlooks the scene. An old wharf on the offside was once the local council's rubbish disposal point. Refuse boats worked down the canal from Paddington collecting from various locations. They then went in convoy to tips at West Drayton and Cowley to be reloaded with sand or clay to return to Paddington.

A traditional humpback canal bridge leads to the moorings of the West London Cruising Club. After this the slopes of Sudbury Golf Course and Horsenden Hill appear on the offside and flowers from gardens spill over on to the towpath as the canal takes on a distinctly rural aspect.

   The Horsenden Farm Visitor Centre has a shop, café and picnic area by the waterside. A public trip boat operates from the newly constructed wharf. The entrance is at Ballot Box Bridge just beyond the golf course. At Ballot Box Bridge energetic walkers can take a diversion to see the fine view from the summit of Horsenden Hill.

A walk up Horsenden Hill

   Leave the canal and cross Ballot Box Bridge. Pass the entrance to the Visitor Centre and turn right by the information boards. Go straight ahead, following a steep path uphill through woodland. At the top, turn left and walk along to the summit of the hill. There are further information boards at the top, where you can enjoy superlative views from the highest point in west London. There are several other walks around the hill to be enjoyed before returning to Ballot Box Bridge *(from where Perivale station can be reached about a quarter of a mile down Horsenden Lane)*. Note the tie-beams on the bridge with the canal company's initials and the year 1909.

Canoeists at Ealing Countryside Weekend, Horsenden Hill, Paddington Canal.

   On the towpath side is Perivale Wood, one of the oldest nature reserves in Britain. Established in 1902, it is an ancient oak wood, rich in bird life and wild flowers. It is managed by the Selborne Society, which hosts an open day in May for visitors to see the bluebells. The tree has become a symbol for the London Borough of Ealing, which has a very active open-space and countryside department.
   With thick woodland on one side and fields leading up to Horsenden Hill on the other, you get the feeling of being out in

Moorings by Northolt Mosque, Paddington Canal.

the countryside. An elegant footbridge gives you an alternative route to Horsenden Hill across wide open fields, often ablaze with buttercups in the springtime. Another diversion can be taken into Paradise Fields on the towpath side. This is a wetland nature reserve created by Ealing Council with lakes and areas devoted to wild flowers. Westway shopping centre can be reached through Paradise Fields.

Industry returns after Greenford Road Bridge with the pleasant smells of a bakery before the canal reaches the Black Horse pub at Oldfield Lane. *Greenford station (Underground, Central Line; National Rail from Paddington) is just a short distance beyond the pub*, which has a large canalside garden. Soon afterwards the towpath climbs steeply over the entrance to Lyon's Dock. This was the last private dock to be built in London (in 1922) and was constructed with materials brought by boat. In its commercial heyday large quantities of coal, tea and oil were carried into the dock. Soon after its construction the dock received a royal visit by King George V and Queen Mary, who came to inspect the new mechanical equipment used to unload the barges. At the time the factory had the largest tea-packing plant in the world. In 1926 the company expanded its site to the opposite side of the canal, where a new factory called Bridge Park began manufacturing ice-cream. The ice-cream business was eventually sold in 1992 and the main factory had been sold and demolished by 2002. In 2004 the dock was standing rather forlorn amid a huge building site.

Lines of linear moorings begin after the iron railway bridge that carries the Central Line trains of the London Underground. This leads to the High Line Yachting boatyard and the Northolt Mosque. From this bridge you can walk to St Mary's Church, Northolt (*Northolt station: Underground, Central Line*).

A walk to St Mary's Church, Northolt

Cross the bridge between the mosque and the boatyard. Follow the path across a road and on through woodland. At the end, turn left into Court Farm Road, which leads to a pleasant little green with a stream running through it and a pub on the right. Turn left and left again opposite the Crown pub. This takes you up to the thirteenth-century St Mary's Church on the hill. There is a gap in the hedge opposite the church door that leads to a path downhill and back to the canal.

St Mary's Church, Northolt, Paddington Canal.

St Mary's Church and its surroundings are part of the Northolt and Greenford Countryside Park. This extends for some distance beyond the A40 Western Avenue and is bisected by the canal. It incorporates parkland, a golf course, playing fields and former scrubland. A new footbridge over the canal just beyond Western Avenue links Marnham Fields to the rest of the country park. Altogether there are 270 acres (109 hectares) of open space managed by Ealing's Parks and Countryside Service.

There is a pub near the canal at Ruislip Road called the Civil Engineer, named in honour of the Taylor Woodrow offices that occupied both sides of the canal. The pub remains but the offices have gone and in 2004 a residential project called Grand Union Village was being built on the site.

A fine piece of landscaped parkland leads to a handsome footbridge that carries the Hillingdon Trail footpath over the canal. The entrance to Willowtree Marina is just beyond the bridge. The marina has two basins for boat mooring and is attractively situated in an area that once contained the Hayes brickfields. Willowtree Marina has all facilities for resident and visiting boaters plus a bistro restaurant and wine bar.

Three substantial arms led off into the workings and in later years, when the fields were worked out, the rubbish boats from Paddington used the docks. One of the arms, called Yeading Dock, had incinerators for burning rubbish. In the end it could not cope with the vast amounts coming in by boat, so the rubbish was buried in the ground.

Spikes Bridge, which has been rebuilt, links housing estates on either side of the canal. Offside moorings are followed by a row of modern houses while on the towpath side Territorial barracks lead up to the Uxbridge Road Bridge in Southall. There are shops and a wide choice of Indian restaurants, reflecting the large local Asian population. Buses go to Uxbridge in one direction and Ealing in the other. The Hamborough Tavern is by the canal bridge and there are numerous factory units and offices in the vicinity. *To reach Southall station (National Rail from Paddington) turn left along The Broadway into the town centre, then at the Old Town Hall turn right along South Street to the station.*

The final mile was once dominated by a series of arms leading off on the towpath side. One of these was the arm leading to Kearley & Tonge's jam factory, known to boatmen as the 'Jam 'ole', which has now been filled in. It was one of the last places in the London area to receive regular supplies of coal from the Midlands by narrowboat. It was the last arm before Bulls Bridge and the junction with the canal's main line. In its place on the industrial estate are roads with such names as 'Trident Way' and 'Boeing Way'. Standing on the Junction Bridge, one needs no reminders of civil aircraft – the proximity of Heathrow Airport is only too apparent.

Willowtree
Marina,
Paddington Canal.

The Regent's Canal

In 1802, a commercial speculator named Thomas Homer, who already had canal interests, had the idea to drive a canal through the centre of London. Even in those days the cost of land in central London was prohibitive so Homer looked towards Marylebone Park on the northern outskirts of the city, where the architect John Nash was building what would become Regent's Park. Homer consulted Nash and suggested that the proposed canal should run through his park. Nash was enthusiastic and subsequently became the driving force in the construction of the new canal. An Act of Parliament was passed in 1812 for a canal from the Thames at Limehouse to Paddington. The Prince Regent had consented to the new park being named after him, and so the canal eventually took his title as well.

Nash wanted the canal to go through the middle of the park but the Crown Commissioners objected. It was thought that working boats and their crews would lower the tone of such a fashionable place of recreation. The canal was therefore

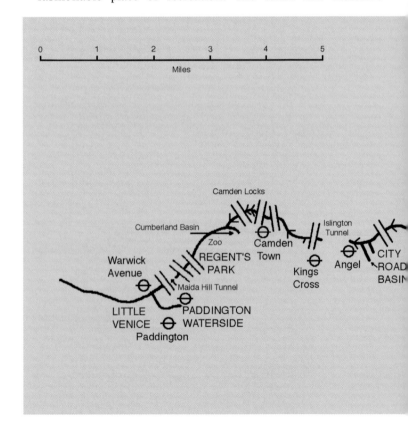

banished to a cutting in the northern fringe of the park. It was soon beset by more problems. An intransigent landowner named William Agar objected to the canal and forcibly defended his property against the navvies. The engineer James Morgan, who was put in charge by Nash, had no canal experience and made mistakes at several places, including the tunnels. To add to these difficulties, Thomas Homer embezzled most of the company's funds. He was eventually arrested, tried and transported. Despite all these problems the 8$^{1}/_{2}$ mile (14 km) canal opened in 1820. It is a wide canal built to carry heavy-laden barges and has two tunnels and twelve locks. Unfortunately the canal arrived too late to be a complete financial success, as railway competition was soon felt. In 1845 a consortium was founded to convert the canal into a railway but financial constraints and opposition from the Grand Junction Canal Company saw the scheme collapse.

The Regent's Canal begins at Little Venice (see page 24) (*nearest station Warwick Avenue: Underground, Bakerloo Line*). On the left by the Warwick Avenue Junction Bridge is Junction

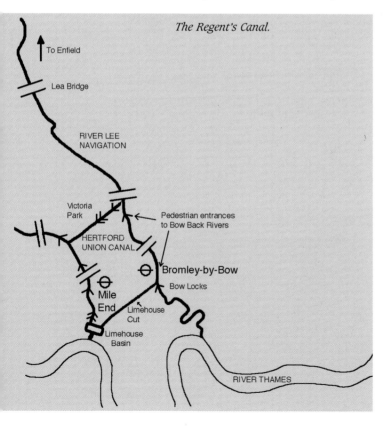

The Regent's Canal.

House. This was once the toll-house for the Regent's Canal. Lines of colourful moored boats lead the canal to Maida Hill Tunnel. The towpath is not accessible so you must walk along Blomfield Road or Maida Avenue, both parallel to the canal. Note the blue plaque on a large house in Maida Avenue close to the tunnel entrance. This was the home of the actor Arthur Lowe, best known for his memorable portrayal of Captain Mainwaring in *Dad's Army*.

The 272 yards (249 metres) long Maida Hill Tunnel has no towpath so in the days before engine power, boats had to be 'legged' through the tunnel while the horse was led over the top. Legging involved the boatmen lying on their backs on planks and driving the boat through the tunnel by 'walking' along the tunnel wall. A café directly above the tunnel has wonderful views of the boats passing below. This could have been the site of Lord's Cricket Ground if the canal had not been built on the land that Thomas Lord had originally intended for the stadium. Compensation was paid and Lord built his cricket ground in its present situation, using soil excavated from the tunnel.

Walkers must follow the path of the boat horses, crossing the busy Maida Vale into Aberdeen Place. Walk to the end of the road and opposite a pub you will see a sign indicating the canal through a gap in the wall. Walk down the steep ramp to the towpath below. There is another short tunnel at Lisson Grove that has a towpath and a house sitting on top of the eastern portal.

Between the two tunnels, boats once unloaded coal at the Marylebone Power Station and took away ashes. All that is left of the site is an anonymous high wall. Beyond Lisson Grove a large housing estate has been built on the old Marylebone railway goods yard. Lisson Green moorings have a long line of colourful canal boats with little gardens on the towpath side. The wrought-iron security gate has decorative ironwork depicting all manner of animals, birds, insects and even a boot and a bottle of wine.

A Regent's Canal signpost, Aberdeen Place, Maida Vale.

Decorative wrought ironwork at Lisson Green moorings, Regent's Canal.

Next we pass under two gloomy railway bridges and the Park Road Bridge into Regent's Park. The contrast is quite extraordinary as the canal is now flanked by a series of handsome mansions with beautifully maintained terraced gardens sweeping down to the water. Added to this scene is the minaret of the mosque at Hanover Gate, which can be seen poking through the trees. Regent's Park, built by John Nash, was completed in its present form around 1827. It was named after the Prince Regent, who later became George IV. In earlier times Henry VIII had used it as a hunting estate.

The canal continues along a wooded cutting on the fringe of the park and parallel with Prince Albert Road. It looks particularly lovely in October when the mature trees display their autumn colours. This is without doubt one of the finest urban stretches of waterway anywhere in Britain.

The second bridge along the cutting, with five supporting pillars on each side, is the celebrated Macclesfield Bridge, known as 'Blow-up Bridge'. Here, in the early hours of 2nd October 1874, the barge *Tilbury*, carrying 5 tons of gunpowder, exploded with devastating results. All that remained of the bridge was a pile of bricks 10 feet (3 metres) high out of the water. Nothing was ever found of the crew of three. Houses were damaged and windows shattered. The effect on the animals at London Zoo was not officially recorded but it is believed that extra wheelbarrows had to be brought into the elephant house!

The original supporting columns were saved and later re-erected when the bridge was rebuilt. They were replaced in reverse so that the original towing-rope grooves worn by the boat horses were set on the wrong side. The columns now have grooves on both sides – one set worn before 1874 and the other set afterwards. The word 'Coalbrookdale' can be seen at the top of the columns. This refers to the town by the River Severn in Shropshire where the supports were cast.

Another fine iron bridge, with an arch and fancy wrought ironwork, leads into London Zoo. The zoo was designed by Decimus Burton and opened its doors to the public in 1828. It has thousands of species of animals in its 36 acres (15 hectares) and is also an important research centre. There is no direct entry to the zoo from the towpath so visitors must leave the canal and follow the signs for the entrance. Terraced antelope paddocks give the animals a fine view of the boats. The angles and corners of Lord Snowdon's soaring aviary overlook the water and dominate the whole scene. The landing stage for the zoo water-buses can be seen just beyond the next bridge, which is an internal footbridge for the zoo. A sloping grassy embankment inside the zoo is covered with daffodils in springtime. During the summer months this section of canal is busy with trip boats and water-buses; the towpath fills with walkers, joggers and office workers enjoying a lunchtime break.

After another iron bridge the canal turns sharply left to Camden Town. Ahead is the foreshortened Cumberland Basin, with moored boats and a floating Chinese restaurant. A canal arm once ran for half a mile to Cumberland Hay Market near Euston station. It was filled in after the Second World War and part of it now supports the London Zoo's car park.

An immediate change of character follows the canal's change of direction. The greenery of Regent's Park gives way to tall residences with colourful gardens visible through a tangle of willow trees. Steps at the next bridge allow access from

Gloucester Avenue. In the days of steam this area was polluted with a permanent pall of smoke from the nearby Euston railway. Trains leaving the station face a steep incline to cross the Regent's Canal and originally had to be assisted by cable haulage.

The medieval-style battlements of the Pirate Castle youth club add an unusual touch to the Camden scene. Opened in 1977, this watersport-orientated club provides recreational facilities for young people in a deprived inner-city area.

A towpath rises steeply over the entrance to a subterranean arm that disappears under a large warehouse. This was a canal-to-railway interchange where wines and spirits were loaded from underground vaults. It was known by some locals as the 'Camden Catacombs' and by others as 'Dead Dog Tunnel'. An elegant roving bridge that transfers the towpath to the opposite side of the canal frames the Hampstead Road Locks. These locks bring to an end a 27 mile (43 km) lock-free pound from Cowley on the Grand Union main line (see page 19). Underneath the bridge there is an old winch that once worked a lock gate by the River Lee at Limehouse. The Greater London Industrial Archaeology Society moved it here in 1968 after the lock closed down.

From the top of the bridge a good view can be had of the double locks now surrounded by what is probably the most cosmopolitan market in Britain. Camden Lock Centre opened in 1973 around a complex of old canal buildings that included a timber-yard and stables. The colourful scene contains shops and stalls selling a huge variety of goods. Exotic scents from

A busy day at Camden Lock, Regent's Canal.

cosmopolitan restaurants mingle with burning incense and smells of more dubious origins. The popularity of Camden Lock Centre is underlined by the spread of the market into neighbouring streets. It has become one of the main attractions for visitors to London looking for something a bit more outrageous than the usual traditional tourist sites. The castellated lock-keeper's cottage later became an information centre but has now found a new lease of life as a coffee house. Behind it a pub with waterside seating and a new hotel have transformed this side of the locks. The *Jenny Wren* trip boat is based at Walker's Quay next to Camden Road Bridge. It runs regular trips to Little Venice. *Jenny Wren* has a waterside restaurant and a restaurant boat is available for hire. The London Waterbus Company's boat service starts from the short arm in Camden Lock market with trips to Little Venice. *The nearest station is Camden Town (Underground: Northern Line)*.

Hampstead Road Locks are the only paired locks that are still in use. All the rest have been reduced to singles with the second chamber blocked off or cascaded. The towpath changes sides again after the top lock, so cross the bridge but do not cross the road unless you want to visit the market extension. A ramp will return you to the towpath, where, continuing eastwards, you will soon pass by Hawley Lock and Kentish Town Lock. The canal winds between high office buildings and under several bridges. One bridge has a canalside pub called the Constitution with a colourful painting on its wall. Horse ramps can be seen at intervals. These sloping brick ramps set into the towpath were constructed to help horses escape from the water if they fell in. Some boatmen used the ramps to wash their horses – much to the annoyance of the canal company.

The next section passes through the once notorious Agar's Town, named after the landlord William Agar, who objected to the canal being built across his land and was duly compensated. Agar's Town was an insalubrious slum of squalid, confined tenements that mostly disappeared when the Midland Railway was built through it. The railway passes over the canal on a tunnel-like bridge. Beyond it the canal opens out, revealing St Pancras Lock and St Pancras Basin, home of the St Pancras Cruising Club. Originally the basin was a coal wharf for the Midland Railway Company. Beyond the lock, on the offside of the canal, is Camley Street Natural Park, opened in 1985 and managed by the London Wildlife Trust. This welcome strip of greenery is overlooked by a brooding group of gasholders. The neo-Gothic spires of St Pancras station, the gasholders and the Post Office Tower present a dramatic backdrop to the lock. This area of St Pancras is set to be transformed by the Channel Tunnel Rail Link project: a new bridge will be built for the railway, crossing the canal between the old St Pancras Midland Railway viaduct and St Pancras Canal Basin.

The canal widens out just before Maiden Lane Bridge at York Way. This is the point at which tunnels carrying the main King's

Cross railway pass under the canal. During the Second World War gates were installed by the bridge as a precaution to prevent the canal flooding the railway tunnel if it were bombed. *Turn right at the bridge for King's Cross stations (National Rail and Underground, Circle, Hammersmith & City, Metropolitan, Northern, Piccadilly and Victoria Lines).*

After the bridge, Battlebridge Basin comes into view. This is the home of the London Canal Museum, housed in a former ice-cream warehouse built in the 1850s by Carlo Gatti. Blocks of ice were imported from Norway and carried from Limehouse by canal boat. Ice wells beneath the warehouse have been excavated and are on view to the public. The museum tells the story of the development of London's canals and the people who worked the boats in its commercial heyday. Among the many wharves and yards bordering the basin was that of Dickinson's paper mills, one of the great patrons of the Grand Union Canal. Boats brought paper from the canalside mills in Hertfordshire and reloaded with wood pulp and other raw materials for the return journey. Battlebridge is the old name for King's Cross and the basin has moorings for numerous canal boats. There is a waterside pub in the basin opposite the museum. Visitors for the museum should turn right over the next bridge and then right again and left into New Wharf Road. There is no direct towpath access to the museum.

Back at the towpath, the gaping mouth of Islington Tunnel ends this section of canalside walk. The tunnel is 960 yards (878 metres) long and has no towpath. As at Maida Hill, boats had to be 'legged' through this tunnel until 1826, when they were towed through by steam tug working on a continuous chain fixed to the canal bed. It is possible to see light at the other end of the tunnel. On some earlier tunnels in other parts of Britain primitive surveying methods left kinks and curves, making it impossible to see the other end on entry. Walkers have to follow the footsteps of the boat horses to the other end of the tunnel. Horses went over the top, often in the charge of the boatmen's children. Today's walkers can follow a waymarked trail with watery symbols on the pavement.

At the top of the tunnel, cross the road and join a path that leads between the flats. Pass a school and turn right into the main Barnsbury Road. Cross the road in front of a church to the pub opposite. Follow Chapel Market along the right-hand pavement to the end of the road and turn right. At the T-junction with Upper Street cross over to *Angel station (Underground, Northern Line)*, then turn left away from the station and take a right turn at the pub on the corner of Duncan Street. Follow the street to its end, where you will see a gap in the railings opposite. This brings you down to the eastern portal of Islington Tunnel.

Islington Tunnel opens out into a tree-lined cutting flanked by smart terraced houses with well-kept gardens. A line of moored boats leads to City Road Lock, where in 2004 a residential development was being constructed by the bottom of the lock.

The wide expanse of City Road Basin has a backdrop of the City of London skyscraper buildings. In 1820, Pickford's Carriers had 120 boats and four hundred horses working out of City Road Basin. When the company ceased trading here it was replaced by the renowned canal carriers Fellows, Morton & Clayton. The City Road wharves continued to be busy beyond the Second World War. At the start of the twenty-first century canoes and sailing boats provide the only sign of life in the old basin, which has been awaiting major development for some time. It is the home of the Islington Boat Club.

Wenlock Basin, smaller than City Road but important in the canal's commercial heyday, is a short distance away. It is overlooked by tall office buildings and is used for offline moorings. The Narrow Boat pub is opposite Wenlock Basin.

The towpath area between the Narrow Boat pub and Sturt's Lock has been pleasantly landscaped with shrubs and seating for walkers. There is a group of office boats moored by Sturt's Lock. More of these boats are planned for the redevelopment at Paddington Basin.

Joggers on the Regent's Canal near Sturt's Lock.

The towpath rises over the arm to Kingsland Basin, which has a few boats on its moorings but is looking rather forlorn and

unkempt. A smaller basin at Laburnum Bridge is next to a school and is used by a community boating centre. The bridge and surrounding walls are adorned by a series of colourful mosaics made by the schoolchildren with official approval.

Passing Acton's Lock, you are entering a part of the canal described in the nineteenth century as a lawless area. Judging by the security grilles on windows and doors of today's houses one can assume that not much has changed. A towering gasometer leads to Mare Street Bridge, with the black hole of a long-forgotten canal arm on the offside of the canal. *Cambridge Heath station (National Rail from Liverpool Street) is nearby.*

Very soon the green oasis of Victoria Park comes into view. It was opened in 1848 and is by far the largest open space in London's East End. Over the years it has provided a welcome area of recreation and has been the setting for a number of political rallies. It has a large lake that is studded with islands bright with rhododendrons in the springtime. A wild deer-park in London's East End comes as something of a surprise but there are also more conventional facilities such as a café and playing fields.

On the left, after Old Ford Lock, is the entrance to the **Hertford Union Canal**. Also known as 'Duckett's Canal', this provides a short cut to the Lee Navigation avoiding the trek down to Limehouse Basin. The canal was built in 1830 by Sir George Duckett and is dead straight for 1½ miles (2.5 km), with three locks. Victoria Park provides an attractive boundary for much of its length. The rest has a mixture of new housing and crumbling old factories. Imported timber for the furniture factories on the River Lee was an important commodity on the Hertford Union. Some years ago a company wanted to keep large tanks full of live eels in the canal – jellied eels are a local delicacy in the East End – but permission was refused. Back at the Regent's Canal, Bow Wharf is a modern development by the junction, with restaurants, bars and boutique shopping.

Canary Wharf, looking like a rocket ship about to go into orbit, and its attendant skyscraper buildings bring a feeling of Manhattan South to the backdrop of Mile End Lock. A new park with lakes and natural wildlife areas has been created in an intensely built-up area. Even on the canal there are swans, coots and mallard ducks, all thriving in this most unlikely place for wildlife. *Mile End Underground station (Central and District Lines) is close by the park.*

A canopied warehouse at Sutton Wharf once allowed boats to load timber under cover.

The Ragged School Museum appears after the desolation around Johnson's Lock. The museum spreads over three Victorian warehouses and was once a free school set up by Dr Barnardo for poor children. It is now a museum of East End life run by volunteers and has a towpath café and shop.

Beyond Mile End Stadium, an isolated chimney stands by the towpath but the factory it once served has long gone. A ramp and footbridge have brightened up the environs of Salmon Lane

Limehouse Marina at Limehouse Basin.

Lock. Factories and offices rear up on both sides and at Commercial Road Lock one gets the impression that the canal is the only place that is no longer commercial.

Limehouse Basin, formerly Regent's Canal Dock, was built in 1820. Produce and raw materials from all over the world were loaded into canal boats for distribution throughout England. The dock also exported all manner of produce and remained active until the late 1960s. Over the years it was enlarged five times and in 1876 2.25 million tons of coal were unloaded. The old Limehouse Locks leading into the Thames were closed in 1968 and a new section of canal was built to connect Limehouse Cut to the dock. A broad tidal lock was constructed with direct access to the dock, but all this enthusiasm was short-lived as the dock was closed to shipping by 1970. Commercial activity ended and gave way to recreational use. The cranes stood collecting rust and an air of dereliction prevailed for many years. What you see now is an amazing transformation, with the old dock surrounded by modern housing in keeping with the development of the rest of Docklands. The water space has become Limehouse Marina, filled with a variety of canal and river craft. The Cruising Association has its headquarters opposite an octagonal cabin that controls the tidal lock. The Hydraulic Accumulator Tower is one of the few old buildings still surviving in the dock. It was part of a pumping station built in 1869 that had its engine and boilers beneath the railway arches that now carry the Docklands Light Railway.

Limehouse station (National Rail from Fenchurch Street; Docklands Light Railway from Bank and Tower Gateway) is nearby.

The Lee

The **Limehouse Cut** was built in 1770, long before the Regent's Canal. It is about a mile long and connects the River Lee Navigation to Limehouse Basin and the Thames, avoiding the winding loops of Bow Creek. It is a wide, straight canal that passes through an intensely built-up area. It was once shut away from public access but now British Waterways has a programme to improve the towpath and make the local public aware of the waterway. The floating towpath under the A12 road at Bow Locks is an excellent innovation that has solved the problem of public safety, crossing under a very busy road where no towpath previously existed.

The **River Lee Navigation** begins at Bow Locks, where boats can enter or leave the tidal Bow Creek.

Navigation on the Lee dates back to Roman times. Most of London's grain came from the region around Ware and so an Act was passed in 1571 to speed up the journey between Ware and London by making an artificial channel. The new navigation was completed in ten years. Later the Lee had an additional role in providing drinking water to the capital, supplementing the New River, which had been supplying spring water to London since 1613. Improvements to the navigation were made as the years progressed. In the 1920s it was considerably enlarged so as to allow 130 ton barges through to Enfield and 100 ton craft to Ware. Increased traffic led to bottlenecks and so some of the locks were mechanised and duplicated. Timber for the furniture industry was one of the principal cargoes on the Lee but trade eventually diminished and regular freight traffic ended around 1984.

The Lee Valley Regional Park was established in 1966 and stretches for 26 miles (42 km) along the banks of the River Lea. (The confusion over the alternative spellings 'Lee' and 'Lea' is usually explained by the use of 'Lee' for the navigation and 'Lea' for the natural river.) The park includes 10,000 acres of recreational space. The Lee Valley Pathway launched in 1996 provides a 28 mile (45 km) pedestrian and cycle way from rural Hertfordshire to the River Thames.

An interesting tour along the Lee starts at Bow Locks. The nearest station is *Bromley-by-Bow (Underground, District Line)*. A long footbridge crosses the towpath over the locks. Look behind you for a splendid view of the Canary Wharf building on the Isle of Dogs. Just beyond the railway bridge is an entrance to the **Bow Back Rivers**. These are a 5 mile (8 km) maze of semi-tidal channels between Bow and Stratford. They were heavily silted with two impassable locks. The rebuilding of Bow Locks will hold back all but the highest tides and should stop the channels from silting up too quickly.

The Channel Tunnel Rail Link, which is to open at nearby

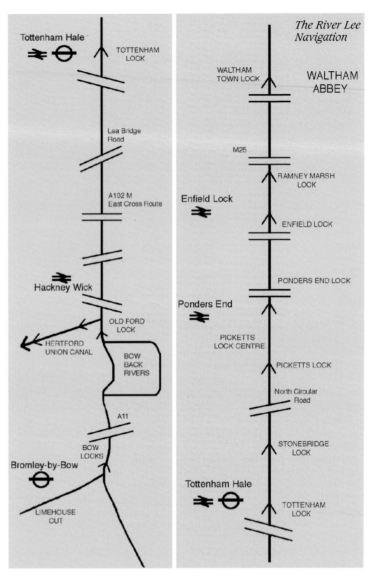

The River Lee Navigation

Stratford in 2007, and a possible 2012 Olympic Games in London's East End have put the spotlight on these muddy backwaters. Their development potential has been realised and various proposals are being put forward to turn the Bow Back Rivers into a boom area such as Docklands. Footpath access is best from Old Ford Lock.

Three Mills is a gem of industrial architecture and is one of the finest groups of waterside buildings in London. The House Mill, built in 1776, is the oldest and largest tidal mill in Britain. It used to grind grain for gin distilleries and the public can see its milling machinery and waterwheels. The House Mill is open to the public on Sunday afternoons from May to October and has guided tours. The Clock Mill (1817) has a timepiece in the tower, making it the most prominent of the Three Mills complex. The tide mill worked by allowing tidal water to flow upstream but holding back the ebbing water by use of floodgates. When the downstream water level dropped, the floodgates opened and the onrushing water turned the mill wheel. The third mill was probably a windmill that has long gone. Three Mills also contains a film studio that is not open to the public. There is a large waterside Tesco supermarket opposite Three Mills.

Continuing northwards, the towpath suddenly comes to a stop at the A11 Bow Flyover. A floating towpath similar to the one at Bow Locks is a possibility for the future but for the present it is necessary to cross the busy road to rejoin the towpath on the other side. Almost immediately, cross over one of the entrances to the Bow Back Rivers. This is the City Mill River, which is accessible for boats but has no footpath at this point. It is possible to see some of the Bow Back Rivers from an elevated footpath called the Greenway (look for a sign immediately before the Northern Outfall Sewer Bridge). Direct towpath access can be had just before Old Ford Lock. From here it is possible to explore most of the Bow Back Rivers on foot.

Old Ford Lock (not to be confused with the one on the Regent's Canal) used to be the headquarters of *The Big Breakfast* television programme and the lock house had a very colourful garden with a giant teacup. Sadly, this has gone and the premises are being redeveloped. In the summertime this section of the Lee Navigation can be badly affected by floating duckweed, which can make the water surface resemble a bowling green. The junction with the Hertford Union Canal appears on the left soon after the lock. Nearby is *Hackney Wick station (National Rail, North London Line)*.

Hackney Stadium, on the right beyond the towpath, has been empty and disused for some years. Its future may well depend on London's bid for the 2012 Olympic Games. Two pleasant new housing estates lead to Hackney Marshes. The area was set up as a public open space in 1894 and many famous footballers developed their skills on the numerous pitches.

The towpath changes sides twice before and after Lea Bridge Road, where there is an Ice Centre. Walthamstow Marsh Nature Reserve covers several acres and is a Site of Special Scientific Interest. A large housing estate with a waterside pub faces the nature reserve. This leads to Springfield Park and Springfield Marina. The river is often busy with rowing boats from the Lea Rowing Club, which has an adjacent waterside café. Springfield Park is a popular spot for walkers, joggers and people who just want to sit and watch the boats go by.

A boat entering Stonebridge Lock, Lee Navigation.

The Beam Engine Museum at Markfield Park has a restored engine that has been working here since 1886. Unfortunately, the fine Grade II listed building has been badly defaced by graffiti.

The first of the thirteen Lea Valley reservoirs is situated opposite Markfield Park. The reservoirs supply 10 per cent of London's water and stretch for 7 miles (11 km) between here and Enfield.

A waterside pub called the Narrow Boat sits among new housing before Tottenham Lock. *Tottenham Hale station (Underground, Victoria Line; National Rail from Liverpool Street) is nearby*. The nearby reservoirs are important bird reserves. After Tottenham Lock the navigation takes on a more rural aspect as it passes Tottenham Marshes. Stonebridge Lock is pleasantly situated despite the attendant electricity pylons. At the car park there is a series of interesting mosaics made by local schoolchildren. Moorings stretch alongside the navigation on both sides of the lock. It is very popular with fishermen, which is not surprising on a river made famous by Izaak Walton's *The Compleat Angler* (1653). The towpath changes sides at Stonebridge Lock and passes under the Lea Valley Viaduct. This part of Edmonton was the centre of a thriving furniture industry with timber-yards and factories alongside the navigation.

At Picketts Lock, the Lea Valley Leisure Centre has a golf course, camping site and a large undercover recreational complex that includes twelve cinemas. Unfortunately, there is no mooring for boats and no bridge for pedestrians from the towpath. Picketts Lock is a single lock that was never converted to doubles like the others on the navigation. It is flanked by a huge reservoir popular with bird-watchers.

South Island Marina is on a short arm before Ponders End Lock. *Ponders End station (National Rail from Liverpool Street) is a short distance to the left.* A large pub and restaurant called the Navigation looks as if it were built on the site of old maltings. The Brimsdown Business Park now dominates the offside of the navigation all the way to Enfield Lock with another enormous reservoir on the towpath side.

British Waterways has offices and a maintenance yard at Enfield Lock. The local pub is called the Rifles after the famous Royal Small Arms Factory that manufactured the Lee Enfield rifle used by British soldiers in the Second Boer War and the First and Second World Wars. The factory closed some years ago

The Dock at Enfield Island Village, formerly the Royal Small Arms Factory.

and is now the Enfield Island Village, which can be reached by the new Ordnance Road Bridge. It is worth a walk around the Village, where you will find lots of evidence and information about its earlier existence.

The canal continues to Ramney Marsh Lock with its attendant cruising club and moorings. After the M25 motorway the canal approaches Waltham Abbey, where there is the Hazlemere Marina, a waterside pub called the Old English Gentleman and Waltham Town Lock. There is a lot of green open space here and it is an appropriate place to end the walk. *Turn left along Station Road to reach Waltham Cross station (National Rail from Liverpool Street).*

A walk to Waltham Abbey

With your back to Waltham Town Lock, turn left along the main road. The entrance to the Royal Gunpowder Mills is immediately on your left. Explosives have been made in buildings spread throughout its 175 acres (71 hectares) since 1665. It has its own internal canal system among woodland. It is now a Site of Special Scientific Interest (SSSI) and is home to the largest heronry in Essex. The mills are open to the public daily from May to October.

Cross the road and keep going straight ahead towards a roundabout. The Abbey Church is now visible; proceed along Highbridge Street to the entrance. The Abbey Church was founded in 1030 but only the Norman nave and aisles still remain. The gardens are reputed to have been the burial place of King Harold after the Battle of Hastings in 1066. The Greenwich Meridian Line passes through a specially planted rose garden. The Lee Valley Information Centre is in the abbey grounds and the Cornmill Meadows Dragonfly Centre is nearby. There

Waltham Abbey Church.

are plenty of pubs, cafés and tearooms in the vicinity of the Abbey Church.

Some other London waterways

A rash of speculative canal building took place at the beginning of the nineteenth century, following the success of earlier canals. Many grandiose schemes proved to be financial failures and London had its share of unsuccessful waterways, now abandoned.

The **Croydon Canal** was part of a scheme to link London Docks with Portsmouth. Opened in 1809, it left the Thames by Surrey Docks and had twenty-eight locks in the first 5 miles (8 km) from Deptford. It reached Croydon at a point now occupied by West Croydon station. In parts it was a pretty canal but commercially it was a failure. The company sold out in 1836 to the railway company, which laid its track along the route of the canal. All that remains is a short stretch in Betts Park, Anerley.

The **Grand Surrey Canal** opened in 1810 from the Thames to Camberwell with a later branch to Peckham. It has totally vanished under road and building schemes.

The **Grosvenor Canal** left the Thames east of Chelsea Bridge and ran for half a mile to a basin. The canal extended an existing creek and became navigable around 1824. It carried coal and stone and took away rubbish. The basin disappeared under Victoria station in 1860. Later the canal was shortened to a dock by Chelsea Bridge where rubbish was loaded into barges.

The **Kensington Canal**, built in 1828, ran from Chelsea Creek to a basin where Kensington Olympia now stands. In 1839 it was taken over by the West London Railway Company, which built a line northwards to link with the main line. Both canal and railway were a financial disaster and in less than a year the railway was leased off. The company operated at a loss for twenty years – a railway company without a railway, running a canal. Finally, the canal was converted to a railway between the basin and King's Road, Chelsea. Chelsea Creek is all that is left of the Kensington Canal.

The **Fleet** was a navigable river in the twelfth century and became a canal in the seventeenth. Its problems were continual silting and the ancient local practice of using it as a rubbish dump. It was navigable as far as Holborn and was crossed by several fine bridges designed by Christopher Wren. Nothing remains of the canal and the river is now part of an underground sewer.

The **City Canal** on the Isle of Dogs was built on a huge scale as a ship canal but was only 193 feet (59 metres) long. It was no more than a large dock with a lock at either end. It became part of the West India Docks and is now under the shadow of Canary Wharf.

Conclusion

The image of canals, especially those passing through urban areas, has changed completely over the past few years. In London, commercial use of the canals has virtually finished as far as carrying bulk cargoes is concerned. The factories that grew on the canal banks stopped using water transport in favour of road and rail. Wharves, once busy loading and unloading goods and raw materials, became dusty storage places for pallets and redundant equipment. Soon many manufacturing companies moved their factories out of the capital because of the soaring costs of operating inside London. In many cases they have been replaced by acres of anonymous warehousing or redeveloped for residential purposes.

A few years ago a property adjacent to a canal was not regarded as a saleable asset by most estate agents; now at places such as Paddington and Brentford the canal is an integral part of multi-million-pound developments. Use of the towpath is now encouraged and information boards are springing up everywhere. It is hoped that the public, and children in particular, will be educated to appreciate the asset in their midst and not regard it as a convenient place to dump their rubbish. To this end there is a proposal for an electrically driven floating classroom on west London's canals.

Go out there and see for yourself – there is a wonderful network of waterways just waiting to be explored in parts of London you hardly knew existed.

Further reading

Barton, Nicholas. *The Lost Rivers of London.* Historical Publications, new edition 1992.
Burton, Anthony, and Pratt, Derek. *The Anatomy of Canals: The Early Years.* Tempus, 2001.
Burton, Anthony, and Pratt, Derek. *The Anatomy of Canals: The Mania Years.* Tempus, 2002.
Burton, Anthony, and Pratt, Derek. *The Anatomy of Canals: Decline and Renewal.* Tempus, 2003.
Clayton, Anthony. *Subterranean City: Beneath the Streets of London.* Phillimore, 2000.
Conder, Tony. *Canal Narrowboats and Barges.* Shire, 2004.
Lansdell, Avril. *Canal Arts and Crafts.* Shire, second edition 2004.
Smith, Peter L. *Discovering Canals in Britain.* Shire, fourth edition 1993; reprinted 1997.
Ware, Michael E. *History in Camera: Canals and Waterways.* Shire 1987, reprinted 2003.

Useful addresses

British Waterways, Willow Grange, Church Road, Watford WD17 4QA. Telephone 01923 201120. Website: www.britishwaterways.co.uk
British Waterways (London Office), The Toll House, Delamere Terrace, Little Venice, London W2 6ND. Telephone: 020 7286 6101. Website: www.britishwaterways.co.uk
Inland Waterways Association, 3 Norfolk Court, Norfolk Road, Rickmansworth, Hertfordshire WD3 1LT. Telephone: 01923 711114. Website: www.waterways.org.uk
Jason's Trip, Opposite 60 Blomfield Road, London W9 2PD. Telephone: 020 7286 3428. Website: www.jasons.co.uk
Lea Valley Regional Park Authority, Lee Valley Park Farm, Stubbins Hall Lane, Waltham Abbey, Essex EN2 9EG. Telephone: 01992 702200. Website: www.leevalleypark.org.uk
London Canal Museum, 12–13 New Wharf Road, King's Cross, London N1 9RT. Telephone: 020 7713 0836. Website: www.canalmuseum.org.uk
London Waterbus Company, 58 Camden Lock Place, London NW1 8AF. Telephone: 020 7482 2660. Website: www.londonwaterbus.com
Walker's Quay (Jenny Wren), 250 Camden High Street, London NW1 8QS. Telephone: 020 7485 4433. Website: www.walkersquay.com

Magazines
Canal Boat, 3 The Courtyard, Denmark Street, Wokingham, Berkshire RG40 2AZ. Telephone: 0118 977 1677. Website: www.canalboatmagazine.com
Waterways World, 151 Station Street, Burton-on-Trent, Staffordshire DE14 1BG. Telephone: 01283 742951.
Canal and Riverboat, PO Box 618, Norwich NR7 0QT. Telephone: 01603 708930. Website: www.canalandriverboat.com

56

Index

Page numbers in italic refer to illustrations.